Traumacore

Mackenzie Svarrer

BookLeaf
Publishing

Presentation by *BookLeaf Publishing*

Web: www.bookleafpub.com

E-mail: info@bookleafpub.com

ISBN: 9789358366846

First edition 2023

To my father

Thank you for always supporting

my dreams.

ACKNOWLEDGEMENT

Thank you to Ilya and Javonte, for barging into my office to give me love while I was writing.

A very special thank you to my friend, AJ Grisi, for drawing the cover art for me and for always being excited about my poetry.

INDEX

Disembodied

I hear my mother call me
from her bedroom.

She has many forms:

a hard lump or an indent
pressed into the mattress

Tonight, the blankets are
peeled back

       like an eggshell.

Her sheets have gone cold.

The car is not in the driveway.

Hallway.exe

baby hairs on my neck
stand upright

as I tiptoe through
visual snow.

my hand glides against
wooden wall panels.

empty wall sockets
watch in horror

as the bathroom door
closes by itself.

but something more
vicious than any

ghost haunts this
house at night

and I know
she is not home.

Phenol Tanka

There are no stars in
the sky. I lick the phenol
from a chewed glow stick
and light up my little mouth.
My words become luminous.

Pink Mold

I scrape bubblegum
from bathtub tiles

and suck a gnawed
thumb

my throat, rent with
strep, coughs

       sweet mucus

my baby teeth clink
against the faucet-

little belly,

I have nothing
to feed you.

Saturation

My world is saturated in
that hot pink Barbie hue

Here: my mood ring is
always blue, even when
I've been crying.

Bedroom 404

That tall vantablack
silhouette haunts me

as it lingers

       like an echo

just above the covers
where i hide my head

what's worse
is the slow approach

as my rambunctious
blood cells thrum in

my ears like a gong

only to find that, with
the light on, it is just

a wet towel hanging
on my door

life is this:

and nothing more .

Parasomnia Inherited

There is a ghost in the corner of my eye.
Jittering always and cooing. She lives
in my periphery: a carbon copy of my
mother. When my face is slick with tears
she slides beneath my eyelids.

When I lay paralyzed at night, I can see
her dark hair shroud around my face.
She hollows my bones. My soul leaks
outward. I seep into the sheets until my
body is a husk.

She likes it when I lay on my stomach.
It is easier for her to get in, fill my skin
so she can roam my halls. I get up out of
my body. I walk right through the walls.

Summer Dodoitsu

A cricket crawls into my
swimsuit. My sunburnt nose fills
with chlorine, burning my eyes.
The sky turns fuchsia.

Pizza Time Theatre

a diaper without its baby
floats in the ball pit.

i've skinned my knees on
confetti carpet

enough times to know that
my teeth glow

under the black light.

the water fountain has run dry
like my eyes that have

crusted over.

i'm not allowed to eat the pizza
but the stupid mouse keeps

singing.

Liminal

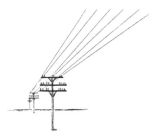

the vacant parking lot
hums a fluorescent hymn.

an icy migraine takes
root in my frontal lobe.

i climb into the backseat.

the tawny glow of street
lights burns itself

onto my retinas. i see life
in after-images. i am
hungry.

we have gone down this
road six times now and
mom won't put the radio
on.

Home Video Rental

I walk down labyrinthine aisles
of DVD shelves surrounded by
piss yellow walls.

The vacant store echoes with
audio feedback as an employee
says the store is closing soon.

I linger at the foreign horror section,
flipping a case over to read the back.
In a few hours, my mouth will be filled
with sour candy.

My body will pump with adrenaline.
I will see shadows in my periphery for
days because horror makes you feel
both awful and brave.

A man is beside me now and
the air is thick with the smell of
spit.

Our eyes meet, he touches me
where he shouldn't and in the long
eternity of a second, my childhood
is flayed off my adolescent bones.
My muscle tissue is exposed to the
elements. I feel putrid. I want my
mommy.

I back away and he nods his head
as if he were greeting me, as if this
all should have been expected.

The Tape (Ringu,1998)

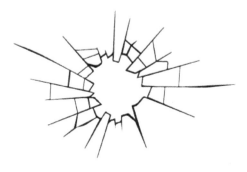

Black clouds haunt a full
moon. Something startles the long-
haired woman brushing
gently in the mirror. Words
creep across the screen like small

beetles. Bodies are
crawling backwards. One man stands
with a shroud in front
of ocean waves. He points at
something (the girl) out of frame.

An eye is staring
back at me. No, it's a well.

The phone is ringing.

Sadako's Somonka

Here I am. Drowning
in murky water, covered
in algae. You watched
the tape my nensha bore. Why
don't you fear my slow trickling?

I don't fear you but
water pours from my soft lips.
Life is full of pain.
I am always waiting to
see a ghost in the mirror.

Maladaptive Daydream

I stare out iridescent
beaded curtains as dark clouds
loom in the sky. The street is
slick with the ghosts of raindrops.

I imagine that beyond
my magenta bedding and
purple lava lamps, the end
is closing in on me with

impending storms. Nephilim
the size of twin towers march
toward the playground. Cheerful
screams become so horrifying.

My empty home becomes a
fortress. I tell myself that
I don't want to die and so,

I cry and cry and cry and-

Tamagotchi

The dawning doom of daylight
Approaches my window as the song of
Morning doves pulls me from my dreams.

Awake, I find my Tamagotchi's
Ghost haunting the keychain.

Only now do I consider the sad truth:
That death is inevitable, no matter how much
Consistent care and love you give something.

How am I supposed to remedy this?
I'll use my earring to press reset.

Untitled Pantoum

i never leave
this endless repetition
this empty mall
haven't I been here before?

this endless repetition
is familiar to me
haven't I been here before?
the hungry void

is familiar to me
this empty mall
the hungry void
i never leave

Suburban Quiet

no one warns you about the
muffled sound that silence
makes

when you are left home
alone at night

the way it coats suburban
houses like a glaze.

it stains the ugly maroon
carpet and ricochets off

vertical rows of oak
wall paneling

you hear the silver jingle of
keys but no one comes
through the door

Dead End

reflective eyes of a doberman
stay trained on me as I teeter

on my bike. my toe grazes
asphalt and I wonder if the

streetlights have multiplied
lengthening the distance to

my house. we are at a standstill.
we are enemies. it doesn't matter

if one of us is more afraid of the other
we're both scared and pissed off at

being stuck in the in-between of

where we were and
where we could be.

Traumacore

Something fuzzy grows on a pile of
laundry in the corner. The carpet is
always damp and smells of mildew.

I address the crayon scrawled on the
wall. His frowny face says, "Don't
come out until morning."

My bedroom window is stuck shut
but I can smell winter wind wafting
through the cracks. My nose drips

like ice. A cold chill silkens my hair as
my tiny fingers pick at old Lisa Frank
stickers on the windowsill.

I can't say what my life has been but
vivianite grows through my skin. Its
pointy shards tear my flesh within.

Ravine Bridge

The ravine below me
bellows like a stomach.

A greedy wind licks
salt from my scalp

and I wonder why
the air is thin

like my mother.

A streetlight spits at me:
You've gained weight!

An autumn chill picks up
somewhere beneath me

and my leather jacket begins
to whine, unable to zip up

any more than this.

Gas Station / Dreamscape

nauseating light bounces
off misty molecules of
almost-rain as

ugly white rays blanket
voyeuristic veils over

dirty gas pumps slick with
petrichor and tar-black
wads of gum

       Glow ghost
       Gas station

my skin is soaked in the
ultraviolet blue of broken

neon signs screaming :

OPEN   OPEN   OPEN

the electric stutter
counts my pulse

and now the word looks
wrong. all pumps remain
empty.

and I don't know if I am
even here or somewhere
else entirely.

Printed in the USA
CPSIA information can be obtained
at www.ICGtesting.com
LVHW020330150224
771724LV00016B/1150

9 789358 366846